# Seeing and Being

## By Chris Dewey

Seeing and Being

Copyright © Christopher Dewey
All rights reserved.

Printed in the United States of America. No part of this book may be used or reproduced in any manner whatsoever without written permission except in the case of brief quotations embodied in critical articles and reviews.

First time or interested authors, contact Fifth Estate Publishers,
Post Office Box 116, Blountsville, AL 35031.

First Printing November 2009

Cover Design by Matt Owens

Printed on acid-free paper

Library of Congress Control No: 2009935156

ISBN: 9781933580739

Fifth Estate 2009

# The Poems

                **page**

**2007**　　　　　　　　　　　　　　　　8

    Whirlwind and the Lotus
    Looking Back
    Walls
    Choices
    Silence
    Nostalgia
    Passion
    Blue
    Implication of Truth
    Full Moon
    A Walk
    Heart Lotus
    Sitting
    Fog
    Demons
    The Great Amusement
    The Great Pain
    Sorrow
    Tiny Moments
    Finding the Elusive
    One Day
    Options
    Blank
    Consequences
    An Undiscover'd Life
    Footprints
    Questions

                                                                    **page**

2008                                                                62

    Path Ahead
    Dark Night
    Childwood
    Making Sense
    Eternal Truth
    Search


2009                                                                74

    Undertow
    One Eye Open
    The Great Answers
    Freedom
    Just Suppose

# Dedication

To fellow travelers who have read these words and marveled at their wisdom:

*"To see a world in a grain of sand,*
*And a heaven in a wild flower,*
*Hold infinity in the palm of your hand,*
*And eternity in an hour"*

*William Blake*

# Prologue

It seems as though my vanity knows no bounds; for here I am once again, offering another volume of 'poetry' to those who might read it. I am not foolish enough to think that my words will be widely read, so to seek to publish a third volume might be considered to be an act of wanton arrogance. I would like to think that I am not alone in my journey, and so I offer my words to anyone with whom they might resonate.

I'm still not sure whether you would call what I write poetic, but if something in what I write does resonate within your soul, then the title of the form matters not in the slightest. After all, it is not 'poetry' that resonates, so much as an idea. As with the two previous books, my poems are sometimes difficult things to read. They sometimes hurt or make us squirm. Sometimes also, they are great gifts of joy, revealing the jokes that we play upon ourselves in our journey towards understanding. They are not delicate morsels for polite conversation, but raw undiluted images from the heart. They are almost always written in the moment as a complete thought. I do not plan them or go through editing gymnastics to render a final product.

As I said in the prologue to both **"Paradox of Being"** and **"Journey into Being"**, writing has always been a catharsis for me and serves as a therapeutic processing mechanism for the activities that occur in the living space between heart, mind and soul. Most of my life has been concerned with asking questions, and I doubt that I am unusual in this. I suspect that most people who search in science or faith, or at the frontiers of any field of human endeavor for that matter, are attempting to answer similar questions. Life is after all, a search for meaning and a search for truth. We understand our ongoing experiences through the filters of what we think we know and what we think we believe, and our perceptions are always colored by their contexts. Writing therefore, helps me to work my way through that labyrinth and whether that writing be in the form of scientific paper, secular newsletter, journaling or poetry, the ultimate goal changes not.

The photography is a balm to my spirit and draws me closer to the essential truth of what is. For me, photography has a Zen-like quality to it. Like most things Zen, however, the more you try to tease it apart, the more it eludes you. As such then, photography is much easier; it occurs as a function of waiting, being patient and being *in* the moment. When I go to nature to take photographs I attempt to become a hole in the universe and let nature happen around me, recording what I see. The images that I keep are those that most closely captured the moment as I perceived it. In a quantum sort of way though, the mere act of observing, changes both the observer and the observed.

Everything is connected. Nothing is ever neutral.

# Seeing and Being

## A Collection of Photographs and Poems

### 2007 to 2009

# The Whirlwind and the Lotus

The whirlwind in a lotus garden:

Frenetic faces fragile.
Storm faces stem.
Power faces petal.

In the garden of the spirit,
The whirlwind spins about,
Thirsting for energy to feed upon,
To succor its survival.

Yet quietly, in the center
Is the peace that is its core.

Within the vortex,
Lies the answer.
Within the beating storm,
Lies its silent heart.

And waiting in the garden,
Is the lotus;
Perfect, mythic,
Precious, fragile.

Is this the source of fear?


05/07

## Looking Back

I stop awhile,
And look over my shoulder
At the road I have walked.

And there you are.
Far in time and space,
And yet
Hauntingly close.

I could reach out and touch you,
But integrity stays my hand.

And so I turn to face my future,
And my heart breaks anew.

I do not understand
Why it is,
That you should be
My other self.
A truer self.
The self I could have been,
Had I not let loose the demons of my soul,
In some wild, deranged search for me.

Yet even so, it would change not one thing.

I walk alone….

        ….I could wish that it were not so

But then it would not be this path…

        ….would it?


06/07

# Walls

**Then**

My words tumbled into the night…
           …and fell away into the dark.
…They lacked the depth of meaning
That was their right.
So I let them go.

**Now**

In this morning there is nothing…
           …but a shadow
Cast across the empty page.
It is not, however, without form.

What I thought was there to write…
           … is something else,
It will come in its own time.
Such is the nature of being.

**Why**

It started with a voice…
An echo, clear and strong,
Across the landscape of my soul;
Shattering the foundation of my walls,
So carefully built by experience of life.

The sound is gone to silence
Its work is done
The walls begin to crack and crumble

And all those bricks,
Laid one upon the next
Will fall to dust…

        …An ample soil for new beginnings.

06/07

# Choices

The air is still,
Here, on the end of the pier.

As I sit beside the lake
I might wish that my mind,
Could mirror its surface.
But I am not the lake.
At least, not now
And my mind…
      …It does not rest.


And yet my thoughts,
Do not disturb the pond,
Or agitate its surface.

So I can be here,
Amid the sounds of nature,
And be still.

For all my inner turmoil,
Peace is still an option.

06/07

# Silence

There is silence here today.
No words to be spoken.
No deeds to be done.

I can rest awhile,
In solitude,
And allow the connection
I feel to Being,
To emerge in full.

There is no need
To dwell on thought,
Or chase the illusions
Of the mind.

They can come and go,
Without comment or restraint.

They are not me.

06/07

# Nostalgia

I lost myself in England
Today…
        …Insofar as I am able.

So many miles.
So many years.

It is a place of my youth,
A place for a child.

Such a place no longer exists,
Except in my mind.

It is place of memories,
Palpable, yet also vague and shapeless,
An intangible, ethereal place –

Where no-one else can go but I.


06/07

# Passion

We wreck ourselves on the shores of passion.
We pour out our hearts to the process of living.
Striving, failing
Loving, falling
It is all, or nothing.
Total commitment to the moments we have.

Barely taking time to breathe or rest,
We throw ourselves into life,
And ultimately into death.

On occasion, when our hearts are open…
In compassion, we see our fellow travelers,
Buffeted about by the storms and tides
Of uncertain fortune;
Bloodied and bruised,
By life,

And we hurt for them.
It is understanding,
Empathy,
Which leaves us thus.

Enlightenment is not about rising above
Or living aloof.
It is about re-entering the ocean of life,
And seeing it for what it is,
And being willing to pay the price…
Time and time again
Without regret or counting the cost.

This is life and this is truly living.

06/07

# Blue

In the dawning moments of your life with us,
In that moment, and in my arms,
Was your beginning
        …but perhaps mine also.

No-one else will ever know,
Nor understand the impact of that moment.

Buried deep within your mind,
You may never know it
        …as a conscious thing.
This thing I can never forget.

I close my eyes,
And see your eyes,
So sure, so strong, so wise.
So blue and
        …so fully alive,
Perhaps, in ways that we forget.

You touched my heart,
And I am not the man I was…

        …my son

07/07

# Implication of Truth

I cannot speak of the truth I know,
For in truth I know it not.
For all my life and all the miles,
What do I know of truth?

It is an interesting thing that honor,
That irreducible empiricist…
Is the arbiter of honest living;
And that integrity
Is an empirical guide of consistent action.

Honor dictates, however,
That the choices of the past
Are indelible,
They have a stony, solid quality;
Not to be erased, but rather, stand
As silent sentinels to truths compromised
And truths defended.
Lessons on the road to wisdom.

So the silent, unread poet,
Writes not merely for self-illumination
But also social contagion…

That lessons learned by one,
            …perhaps,
Might help to heal all.

And yet,
If words fall into dust
And ego drives the motivation
Wherein lies the value of the process?

Could it be
That there is yet more
To see, more to learn
Beyond our oh so certain
View of truth?


07/07

## Full Moon

Silent witness.
Silent shadow.
Silent pond.
Still water.

It is almost daylight,
In this night of the full moon.
My shadow, back lit,
Head in hand,
On the surface of the pond.

But there is no answer here,
Nor in my heart.

God is silent.

Unlike the night.
Unlike my mind.

Tonight there is no solace,
But neither is there fear.

And so I wait.

And continue to breathe.
As the hours tick away.


07/07

# A Walk

We walked awhile…
My heart and I,
Along a dappled path.

A third there was
Our ancient friend.

For Soul came too -
And did for merit's sake,
Not quiet our mind,
Or calm our heart.

In time we stopped,
In summer's shade;
And sweat made do for tears.

We walked awhile…
My heart and I,
And journeyed onward,
Through the wood.

We talked of love,
And talked of hope,
And spoke of dreams untold.

And on we went,
Our little band,
Of Soul and heart and me.

And so once more
When all was done
The mind was calm
And heart was quiet.

We walked awhile…
My heart and I
Along a dappled path.
And faced the truth of life.

08/07

## Heart Lotus

The petals of the heart,
Give themselves
To the sunlight
Of understanding
Only slowly.

Petal by petal,
The Lotus reveals itself;
Each petal seemingly
More beautiful than the last;

Until at its core,
We find the unexpected…

The undiluted truth of self.


08/07

# Sitting

Sitting.
Watching.
Waiting.

Moments drift by.
Insight moves inward,
The world fades away.

Something different emerges.

Reality is something other
Than what we think we perceive.

Neither is the past
What we think,
Nor what we recall.

In likewise fashion,
The future is rarely
What we imagine…
Or that for which we plan.

So we wrestle with Reason
And lose
In the face of the absurd.

Did I see this once before?
Did I once know…
What it is I have lost?
Can I find my way?
Does such a thing exist?


08/07

# Fog

In the fog
Of half-remembered dreams;
Along the moss-covered paths
In the Forest of Events;
Are clues
To something lost.

But it was not always thus –
There was a time before;
But it is not now
And not here…
            That I can see.

So in the rising mists
Of the early dawn,
The pen is still.
And anticipatory ignorance
Waits
For nothing in particular…
Or perhaps it waits
For its own demise.


08/07

## Demons

At some point in the Journey of Life,
We must stand alone
At the graveside of our demons
And lament their passing.

In the deep core of our being
Is an unshed Ocean of Tears
That must pour forth
For healing to occur.

So, as the demons
Are covered with earth
And set to rest;
We must each in our own way…

Give thanks for the lessons offered,
Recognize that there is no undoing the past,
Embrace our wounds,
And wash our scars with our own tears.


09/07

## The Great Amusement

Was it fear or reason that led me here?
Was it the questions I asked?
Or the answers I found?
Was it the demons I let loose?
Or the hope I found?

It really matters not at all.

The simple truth is this:
That in the labyrinth of the mind,
And in the darkest corners of the heart…
The road ahead is back the way we came;
Through the wreckage of the past,
Through the pain and suffering we caused.

In the Quest for Truth,
It is a high amusement
To one day see that the way ahead;
Is to have the courage to turn around…
And go back the way I came.


09/07

# The Great Pain

It is not the crushing, desperate loneliness.
Nor even the aching, unbearable yearning for an end…
        …or a beginning.
It is not even the inability to share that which I feel,
With words that fail as they fall into the yawning emptiness.
It is merely the inability to touch and heal.
And it is the sense of *knowing*
That defies my ability to explain it.

The world of man
Can be a tormented place
Where fractal oceans
Drip like tears
From eyes that have seen too much…
        …and not enough.

It is not the desolation,
Or the void.
It is the certain knowledge
Made only more poignant by those I truly touch
That in my heart,

I walk alone.


09/07

# Sorrow

I feel a deep and structural sadness today;
A sort of rift in reality,
Through which my senses fall…
As I watch, detached, from the edge of Reason.

Perhaps it is the lack of sleep.
Perhaps it is that I lack the strength,
To do battle with my demons.
Perhaps it is that I have yet,
To see the Truth…
For what it is.

But in any event,
Little does it matter.

The sorrow is palpable…
Cavernous and all-consuming.
It wraps about me like a cloak.
I can feel it in the air around me.
It is in my words and in my hands.

I can neither heal the people I touch,
Nor take away the pain I see around me.

And so, that sense of solitude...
Of being so utterly alone,
Is heightened in these moments,
Until finally, it folds in upon itself
And seeks to crush me in its power.

I could scream at the stars
That this is not how things
Are supposed to be.

We are better than this.

But I am lost, and lack the Truth I seek.


09/07

# Tiny Moments

Tiny moments,
Snatched out of time.
Miniature universes,
Full of meaning;
Burned in the memory,
As perceptions of reality.

Are they truth,
As we recall them?
Or merely delusions,
Making life seem more vital,
…Or precious.

You turned around,
And watched me go.
You watched me walk away.

I never knew,
For you never said.

But was it you or I
Who, looking back
Could see the truth
Of what transpired
In that most elusive
Of moments?

Life and all its choices
Hangs on such little things
Such tiny fragments of eternity
Lessons of uncertainty
Missed by most
Ignored by many

The gifts of Life
To those who dare.


10/07

## Finding the Elusive

You asked me once
What is 'elusive'?
I did not give an answer true.

I answer now,
From further down the trail.

....Elusive....

That which is so difficult to catch,
Or to hold.
That which is so easily missed,
When we are not attentive,
Or attuned;
That, which is in plain sight
If we can but open our eyes to see,
But which, so often in our haste,
We miss…
Rather like a sunlit leaf,
On just another branch,
Or a caterpillar on a sodden path.

That which is elusive…
Is so often rich,
So redolent with meaning and value;
But in trying so hard to hold it…
We lose it
...like moving a blade of grass,
To get a better view,
 Instead of leaving things as they are
And being thankful for what is.

Elusive is seeing the true meaning of a thing,
Stripped clear of our desires and wants,
Our prejudices and preconceived notions
Of what we think,
Reality is supposed to be.

Elusive...that, which,
If we do not allow it to be seen,
Is lost for all time...

Such moments come only once,
And their uniqueness can never be recaptured;
No matter what transpires for the rest of time.

....The dew on the flower will never be repeated
In exactly that way again,
No matter how much dew collects on how many flowers
…Thereafter.

....If we do not see
And allow ourselves to be moved
By the celebration of life;
Then that single moment is gone,
As is that single chance.

Life is full of elusive moments,
Why, they are all around us.

Elusive...the ability to see, to feel,
To accept, to learn,
To celebrate, to give thanks,
And to understand
That this universe
In all its forms is a celebration of love…

And to immerse yourself in it,
To swim,
Perhaps to drown a former self
And to be willing…
Even happy to do so,
For such is its gift...

Elusive moments hold the power
To change the world in a single breath.

Elusive moments capture our hearts
And permit us to say 'wow!'
And in the same moment to want to cry
In our exposed humility and awe.

10/07

# One Day

Perhaps,
One day,
When I am no more;
Strange, unknowing hands
Will take a tattered book
From some dusty shelf;
And see within...
Familiar words
That resonate,
That touch the soul
And create a link, within.

And in the mind
That reads the words
Some image of an unlived life
Will grow…

A silent echo
Across the years;

And I shall be loved
Not as I am, or was,
But as some other,
Better self.

And who is to say
That in that moment
The past is not changed
Or formed anew…?

And someone
Whom I never meet,

Will love me
For things I never knew
Existed.

10/07

# Options

Was peace ever an option,
When I chose war?
Was kindness before me,
When I chose pain?

I sit as I was taught
And my heart aches
No less
Than my knees.

And I breathe.
It is all I have.
And even that -
Is not mine,
Is not permanent,
Is not guaranteed.

And so, I laugh.
What other option is there?


11/07

## Blank

There is a blank part of myself,
That if I could turn around and see,
I would understand,
But I cannot and do not.

I journey onward,
Life after life;
Seeking an answer…
Or a key,
To unlock the great mysteries.

I sit in silence,
And let the energy flow,
And in fleeting moments,
Catch a glimpse
Of…

No-thing.

11/07

# Consequences

We search without a map,
In the deep, velvet blackness,
Of spiritual night.

We stumble into other souls;
Who in equal blindness,
Know not really what they touch.

On occasion we are drawn
To a resonant chord,
An echo of some Elysian melody
Known only to the higher self.

It is the quest of living
That we seek to rise above
The physical self;
And aspire to touch…
Perhaps only once in each lifetime,
Immanent nature
And know what truly is;
Rather than that,
Which we pretend exists
From day to day.

But, by that touch
We are forever changed;
Suddenly immortalized
By the awareness
That we need not seek;
For truth is
An inevitable consequence,
Of an honest question.

11/07

## An Undiscover'd Life

There are questions great and small.
There are lives to live;
And there are things
That we each must face,
Within our souls and selves.

It is a discovery of self,
To ask the Great questions,
To attempt with tiny mind;
To tease apart
The deeper meaning,
And find not within the answer
But within the process…
That meanings
Are the contrived tools
Of convenient experience…
Unless perhaps,
We abandon self,
And all its attendant chimerae;

To find the undiscover'd life.

The only one worth living.


12/07

## Footprints

Tide-washed footprints,
Damp, warm sand, bare feet and setting sun,
These are the things of comfort.

I look at the path,
Along the beach,
And feel pulled
Not here…
 …but, rather
Far out to sea.

This is only transient comfort.
Here…on the sand, is
No home for me.

I see the gentle surf,
Wash away my past,
But the sand remembers
As do I.

This is no home for me.

12/07

# Questions

I have often wondered
How it is
That I have come to this place
Of comparative desolation.

I look around me
At the wreckage of my life
And wonder why it is
That we do this with a life.

Why is it
That we take something noble
And pure and honest
And make of it something
Small and petty and ugly?

Why is it
That we walk the paths we take?

Why is it
That we are so blind?

Could it be,
That loving me
Was that worst thing
That you could do?

Could it be
That I ought to live alone?
Hidden, anonymous,
Unknown?

Could it be
That this is how
I should die…
In a place of desolation?


12/07

# Path Ahead

For years I thought
That I was on a path,
That led me to my dreams.

I did not see,
And did not know,
That I made my own path.

There was no path.
There is no path,
That I must follow

There is only the place
In which I choose
To place my foot,
In the next moment
Upon the road of life.

So does it really matter?

There is only one end
Regardless of the paths we choose;
Or how lost we feel,
Along the way.


03/08

# Dark Night

I hear the sounds of my crumbling world
I feel the crunch of rubble underfoot
There are no stars to light my way
And I stumble in the dark
My worn out mind
Finds no rest
And only brief moments of respite
In the acrid smoke of ruin

I feel Death.

It is heavy around me
Waiting
Knowing.

I feel Death whisper
Quietly urging
Subtle, an enticing undercurrent
Beneath the surface of the struggle

And no-one else can see

But I can see his face
And it is my own

And it is merely a matter of time….

….If I allow it.


04/08

# Childwood

I know these woods, these trails
Hidden memories, lost –
Lost within the leaves
Long gone.

These then,
Are not my woods,
Not my trees
They never really were.

Unlike the younger me
I sit in silence,
And feel the years…
The passage of a different time.

Here sits not the boy
Carefree and blind…
Too eager and deaf
To all but the promptings of his heart.

These eyes are not the same
Nor hands, nor ears or mind

But the immortal part
Still resonant within
Remains.
Here in this precious moment
Boy and man sit together
Along the paths of a forgotten past.

06/08

# Making Sense

For years I have been alone
And sometimes in that time,
I have been lonely.

To be one
Is not to be both.

I did not see,
That this is how it is,
For in reality
There is no other choice
When foot touches path.

Only I can walk.
And no one else
Can walk my path;
These are my feet
And my footprints
On the way.


07/08

# Eternal Truth

As on so many occasions,
I sit by the water, beneath the sky
And disappear into nature.

I am become a hole in the universe.
I become one, connected.
I feel the Earth, its pulse, its energy…
Inseparable
And I am therefore,
In a very real sense, not I
Nor other.

Then, in a single moment
Snatched from eternity,
Like an anchor
To keep me present;
The universe turns again
And I see myself in its face
And become again, one,
Unnaturally separated
But never again truly alone,
Isolated or disconnected….

I never was…
      …just me.

09/08

# Search

We search for beginnings at the end.
We search for meaning in the result.
We are blind in the moment,
Because we lack the insight
To see beyond the shell of existence,
That we each create moment by moment,
In our effort to define what is.

To step beyond,
Is an act of faith,
Of courage,
And intent.

And so we cling,
Attached without reason
To the delusions of ignorance.

10/08

## Undertow

I feel the wave ahead,
Though I see it not.

I can feel the beach…
Sucking out from beneath my feet.
Sands of time giving way,
Slipping from between my toes.

I wait,
In the long, slow inhale
Before the storm.

I can face the wave,
Or I can look away.
It makes no difference…

When it passes,
I shall be here still.

But wiser
For the knowing…

If I can hold my footing.


03/09

# One Eye Open

Do we dream with one eye open?
Or live with one eye shut?

Dare we risk to dream of what might be?
While we cling to what we think is?

To truly dream,
Is to abandon the rock of reason;
And allow that the impossible…
Is not.

And,

If, perchance we might awaken,
Are we afraid of what we see?

Do we cling to the delusions
We created?
And in that comfort,
Do we then dream tepid dreams?
And let them go
As fancies of the night?

And when we live in daylight,
Is it really light?
Or are we really half asleep
Afraid to truly wake.


08/09

# The Great Answers

There are questions that we ask,
As we learn and grow;
But they are small and weak,
And do not shake the ground,
Upon which, sure-footed
We erect our banners of truth.

There are other questions,
That give no safety in the asking.

Their answers lie,
As always…
At the frontiers of our lives;
Be they in personal endurance or meditation
Or in science, or in faith
Or yet again in art
Or in the horrors of our wars.

The answers carry all before them;
And we either shrink away,
To some dim-lit corner,
And pretend we never saw;

Or we too are swept away,
To new realities;
And more noble truths.

Where few have been,
And fewer still would choose to go;
This is where the Great Answers lie.

And if you look,
They lie there,
Waiting at your feet.

08/09

# Freedom

When I was young,
I thought that I was free.
But in reality…
(As I look back),
It is just that I was simply
Too naïve, or too selfish,
To see the impact of my choices
Or their consequences,
Upon those I loved.

When I was older,
Looking out from the life I built
And no longer free…
I was, in a sense
Unable to break away
And live as I might once have wished.

So perhaps it is, that…
We create our own chains,
One at a time,
Like silken threads,
Which, if we let them,
Decades later…
Hold us in place
Unable to move.

I see now how blind I have been,
And how dear is the cost of freedom.
I see the price that others pay;
But this is life.
And this is what lies within the balance.

For each of us must live a life;
And pay the toll along the way,
As those we love will pay theirs also.

But to leave a life unlived,
And pathways undiscovered
Would this not
Exact the greater price?

08/09

## Just Suppose

Just suppose
For one tiny instant,
That the Universe,
In all its myriad of forms
Is not the fragmented thing…
That we perceive.

Just suppose,
That all we think we see,
Is merely one
And there is no separation,
No 'other'.

What then?

Just suppose
That for even one microsecond
This tiny mind could grasp…
Or catch a glimpse of…
The full impact of no-things
And the implications of one-thing

What then?

There surely would be silence
In understanding.
For nothing more would need be said
Or done.

For what is, is…

        …And that is enough.


09/09

# Photographs

All the photographs are the work of Chris Dewey and were taken in Canada (Newfoundland) China, Croatia, England and the United States (Alabama, Arizona, California and Mississippi).

## About the Author

Chris was born in England, and received his doctorate in geology while he lived in Newfoundland, Canada. He moved to Mississippi in 1984, where he holds a faculty position at Mississippi State University.

Chris is a mixture of pieces; part scientist, part martial artist, Reiki practitioner, philosopher, poet, amateur photographer and avid reader. He has a deep love for the universe, the environment and for life. It may sound trite, but it is the driving desire to understand life, the meaning of the universe and the nature of the world around him that has led Chris into the life of the geologist, the world of the martial artist, the labyrinth of the poet and the wonder of photography.

Chris has been training in the martial arts since 1968, which coincidentally was shortly before he got his first camera, and was the same year that he decided that he was going to become a geologist when he grew up. He still has not grown up.

As a writer, Chris is published in a variety of venues, both academic and secular. He produces a monthly newsletter entitled *"Pathways"*. He has published a three volume set of books concerning martial arts coaching as well as two other books of poetry: *"**Paradox of Being**"* and *"**Journey into Being**"*.

www.ingramcontent.com/pod-product-compliance
Lightning Source LLC
Chambersburg PA
CBHW041537220426
43663CB00002B/61